The Trial

Transform Your Dating Life In Eight Weeks

By Avery Hayden

Contents:

Introduction: Zen and the Art of Pickup

Section 1: Prepare for Success

Chapter 1: Missed Opportunities

Chapter 2: Self-Help Vs. Reality

Chapter 3: Cupid's Arrow

Chapter 4: Don't Believe the Hype

Chapter 5: The Evolution of Desire

Chapter 6: The Path to Mastery

Chapter 7: You Will Make Excuses

Chapter 8: What You See Is All There Is

Chapter 9: Eight Weeks

Chapter 10: Field Reports Catalyze Change

Introduction:

Zen and the Art of Pickup

It's very easy to make dating advice look stupid. Its most famous figure seems like more of a cartoon than a master of seduction; he introduces himself as Mystery, wears Harry-potter quidditch goggles, a Lincoln top-hat, and asks women what they think of his painted nails (before making them jump through his compliance loops and negging the to lower their relative value).

But Mystery isn't the pickup industry's only oddball. Ross Jeffries created Speed Seduction, which teaches you how to hypnotize women to become sexually attracted to you (this could make for a great how I met your mother story, "Well kids, I used a hypnotic pattern to make her feel submissive towards me...) More recently, the Real Social Dynamics instructor Jeff Allen (known on Okcupid as Captain Derp) got into a minor media scandal for pulling his (apparently small) dick out in his painted 'rape' van.

Not to be outdone, his coworker, Julien Blanc earned the title 'most hated man in the world' and was banned from multiple countries including England and Australia. Why? He gave a speech in which he said picking up girls in Japan is easy, and that you can get away with anything, he suggested that you could grab women by the throat or even better, pull their heads towards your crotch while yelling, "Pikachu!" And he recorded footage of himself doing just that (in his defense, this was all a desperate plea for attention in the form of shock humor, not genuine advice).

Respect the Cock, Tame the Cunt?

From the outside looking in, the pickup community looks like a breeding ground for misogyny, douchebaggery, and a solid dose of asshattedness. To anyone who's never heard of pickup, men involved in the community look like immature adults who never grew up and developed real values, or any respect for the fairer sex. It would be easy to think that these men have a trivial obsession with accruing one-night-stands to prove to themselves in some way. It would seem that Julien Blanc, Mystery, and Dapper Laughs are teaching men how to manipulate and take advantage of innocent women for their own petty desires.

The Surprising Truth

Look, there are some 'sharks' in the pickup community, guys with a classic case of Don Juanism (a compulsive desire to collect notches on their belt). But a recent trend towards self-improvement reveals what pickup is really about at its core. It's a path towards self-acceptance, personal growth, and psychological freedom. The most popular pickup instructors today are teaching pickup as a pathway towards self-empowerment.

It may seem odd that pursuing a goal that is ultimately just pumping some white, viscous fluid into a woman's body might be representative of psychological growth, but that's what the community is focused on at this point.

And although it's odd that modern pickup instructors give speeches about meditation, eastern philosophy, and the law of attraction, there is something valuable to take from this new era of dating advice.

As exciting as the idea of notches on your belt may be, and as fun as it may be to brag to your friends that you just banged an hb9, it's valuable to ask yourself what your deepest motivation is to go on this (easily-parodied) journey towards self-improvement.

Ultimately, the purpose for pursuing pickup is the same as any self-improvement journey whether it be sought through the means of money, fitness, or fame.

Fuck Bitches, Acquire Deep Inner-Fulfillment

We pursue these paths to feel better. Specifically, to feel better about ourselves. And although busting a nut into a hot girl will make you feel better about yourself for a few hours, it's facing your fears and overcoming your insecurities that provides you with the true reward.

Men who are intrigued by the dating advice industry (almost) always have insecurities towards the opposite sex, it's the reason the community is so appealing. If you were totally secure and confident in your interactions with women, it would be unlikely that the dating advice community would interest you, because men who are confident with the opposite sex have no trouble hooking up with women.

These insecurities are the source for some of our deepest emotional pain. Being unable to connect with women not only feels disempowering, but emasculating. Feeling sexually unviable (whether you think it's due to your physical attractiveness or your lack of confidence, or whatever else) is incredibly painful. It's a feeling that we are willing to do anything to overcome.

Sure, pickup is about having sex with women and forming relationships, but beneath that, it's about freeing yourself from a type of mental imprisonment, freeing yourself from feeling helpless because you're too afraid to ask your crush on a date or to lean in for a kiss. Freeing yourself from a fear of rejection that seems like it is controlling your life, and sabotaging your actions. Pickup is about letting go of a tremendous source of pain that has been building up from years of internal struggle.

 Yes, if you follow the blueprint for success The Trial lays out for you, you will get laid, but the real reward is overcoming your insecurities, feeling free from that petrified and cowardly voice in your head that prevents you from taking risks or being vulnerable with women. Nothing is more empowering than transforming from someone who spends his days fantasizing about the adventures and relationships he could have into someone who actually takes the actions necessary to bring his fantasies into reality.

Relationships and sex are fun, but if you focus too narrowly on that aspect of your journey, your motivation will wane over time, because sex isn't going to make you feel good about yourself. You will feel good about yourself when you stop needing sex and emotional validation from women. And approaching women and facing rejection head on again and again is the most powerful and thrilling way to become someone who doesn't rely on others' approval for their own happiness.

If you focus on that as your goal, you will not only become more attractive to women and more capable at building sexual relationships with them. But your relationships won't be focused on emotional validation, but on human connection, which is more enjoyable on every level.

But, if you focus on collecting notches on your belt, you will come to the realization that you still feel empty and unworthy on some deep level, you'll realize pickup isn't working. I've done this, and I've seen a lot of other guys do the same. Dating advice can easily become a bandaid for what is a gaping wound. But pickup can also be something far more empowering when you see it a process of letting go of your self-image, as a process of killing parts of your identity that aren't serving you. Then, and only then, pickup becomes a path towards self-transcendence, a way to free yourself from the emotional treadmill that life can so easily become.

Section 1: Preparing for Success

Missed Opportunities

"Of all the words of mice and men, the saddest are, it might have been" -Kurt Vonnegut

No relationship can make an empty life fulfilling. At the same time, a life in which you cannot connect vulnerably with the opposite sex will always feel empty.

If you were to ask a man on his deathbed what the most important and enlightening aspect of his life was, his answer would almost certainly be his relationship with a woman he loved.

But imagine, he saw her across the room, saw a woman who he was instantly inspired by, but he was paralyzed by anxiety. His heart was screaming out that he needed to meet her, but he couldn't convince his feet to move, he was too terrified by the threat of rejection; a perceived potential for pain motivated him to hesitate. And the story ended there.

Every man who has fallen in love, who has had a meaningful relationship with a woman, at some point had to take a leap of faith, he had to risk rejection. We are constantly reminded of love stories in which a man took that leap; but we never think about the countless love stories that didn't happen because of a man's hesitation.

If you are reading this book, you have already experienced this moment many times. You've had the opportunity to connect with many women who had an immediate and powerful effect on you. And if you had confidently taken the necessary risks, those moments could have led to a deep and powerful connection that would have changed your life.

But, at some point, you got in your own way. Maybe you never approached her, maybe you did, but you didn't make a move because you were afraid to make yourself vulnerable. Maybe you even went on a date with her, but at some point, you gave in to hesitation, and the story ended before it could really begin.

Unfortunately, in your formative years, you picked up beliefs that have damaged your ability to make a real connection with the opposite sex. It's a common occurrence in the modern world, we are raised today to become comfortable in the isolation of our rooms staring at a screen, and uncomfortable with vulnerable self-expression.

Your limiting beliefs have turned what could have been stories of how you found love into stories in which you can only wonder what might have been.

Maybe you're here because you've had your heart broken in a painful toxic relationship, and you want to meet someone better, but it's proven to be difficult.

Maybe you've never been able to connect with the opposite sex romantically at all. Whatever the case, you are among the majority of modern men who aren't getting what they hope for in their relationships with the opposite sex.

But, you are among the minority of modern men who are courageous enough and open minded enough to do something about it. But getting the results you want is going to require that you set your ego aside and prepare to overcome substantial internal resistance to change.

Self-Help Vs. Reality

You picked up this book because you want to make a change in your life, an important change. It takes profound courage to be vulnerable enough to connect with other people, especially members of the opposite sex.

But your conscious desire for change is meaningless unless you can overcome an innate emotional resistance to change that all humans are born with. The part of you that wants to earn an abundant dating life must overcome limiting beliefs, old habits, and emotions that exist to keep you from making positive changes.

Self-improvement books are goldmines for inspiring ideas. But they rarely live up to their promise, they rarely lead to a better life. Why? They are not specifically designed to guide your limited conscious mind towards a distant goal.

They generously dispense interesting ideas, but they don't prepare you for the many obstacles you will inevitably run into. While reading one of these books, you are drawn into a reality of limitless possibility in which you can effortlessly create whatever future you want.

But, put the book down, and you are back in this reality, where change is hard. Self-help books rarely account for this fact, they are not written to guide a limited conscious mind through a difficult and long journey.

The Trial is structured around the fact that change isn't easy, and that there are many obstacles which can lead you to veer off the path. You will be shown the mistakes that you are likely to make before you make them.

Instead of getting inspired by what you should do, and what you should think, you will be shown what change actually looks like with all of its struggles.

You will look through someone else's eyes as they embark on the same journey, and through their perspective you will observe the process of change with all of its blemishes.

Through this unique perspective, you will be able to adapt to each struggle and challenge you will face as it happens. Your conscious mind will still have its many limitations, but you will be guided to your destination every step of the way.

Cupid's Arrow

Infuse your life with action. Don't wait for it to happen. Make it happen. Make your own future. Make your own hope. Make your own love.
- Bradley Whitford

It's comforting to think true love will find you when you're ready for it, that electrifying romance is your birthright as a human being. The widespread idea that cupid's arrow will strike true, so long as you let it, has resulted in a society in which 50% of marriages end in divorce, 70% of people cheat, and a large percentage of men spend months or even years at a time without a woman's touch.

People expect sex and love to happen to them. They treat dating as if success in it was due to fate, rather than skill, as if dating were a game of slots, not a game of chess.

Whether you're reading these pages to find true love or to collect notches on your belt, you must be brutally honest with yourself to make meaningful progress. Having been involved with the dating advice industry for five years now, the patterns have become clear, and they are not encouraging.

Among those who watch seminars, take live programs, or read books, only a minority of men even leave their man cave and venture to environments with fleshand-blood women. Among those who do go out, it is a minority who approach enough women to make meaningful progress, and among them, it is an even smaller minority who are open minded enough and self-critical enough to get the results they want. The guys who take action do get some results, whether it be in the form of phone numbers, make outs, or even the occasional lay, but they tend to get stuck on a plateau, as if they're running on a hamster wheel.

How many men who enter the world of dating advice sleep with women they genuinely consider to be of the highest quality, their dream girls? Almost none. I can confidently say less than 1%. A slightly higher percentage manage to date a girl who they like, but they almost never date the kind of girl they were imagining when they started watching pickup videos. To get results with those women, you must make dating a disciplined practice, which is something few men will ever do.

Don't Believe the Hype

You are not entitled to any success with women. And you're definitely not entitled to success with the highest quality women. The odds are stacked against you. Those who take the socially conditioned path of waiting for cupid's arrow to strike usually find themselves in mediocre relationships which they merely tolerate (for evidence just look to the relationships of people you know). Those who rely on the dating advice industry don't get the easy solution they were promised.

Ask yourself how important this is to you. Can you imagine going without beautiful women in your life? Are you willing to spend hundreds of hours of your time and endure seemingly countless rejections to meet your dream girl(s) and become a man of true self-confidence? If not, don't waste your time, you will only improve your life with this path if you pursue it wholeheartedly.

If you can't imagine living a life without dating women who you find to be both physically stunning and emotionally compelling, then you are in a tough position. You can either settle with a life in which you will endure a steady, gnawing pain because of an unanswered, "what if", or you can live a life in which you will endure the profound pain of changing yourself through learning from rejection to become someone who gets the women you always dreamed about.

The pain of inaction is toxic, but the pain of change is healing: each time you feel humiliated, rejected, or worthless, you have an opportunity to let go of a piece of your ego. As you face your anxieties, you will notice and let go of the many negative thoughts that are holding you back and damaging your self-esteem, and by doing so, improve not only your dating life, but your entire well-being. But to make these changes, you must first look outward, and understand what women want.

The Evolution of Desire

Sexual attraction is nothing more than an evolved emotional response notifying us that a particular individual would be a good candidate to pass on our genes with. When a woman is beautiful you feel physical attraction for her because her beauty indicates that she is fertile and free of disease. Although this perspective might not make for good love poems, looking at attraction from an evolutionary lens allows us to understand what universally attracts women and why. Then, we can reverse engineer those traits to become more attractive ourselves.

Women have a powerful emotional desire for offspring with the best possible genes (better genes mean offspring who are more likely to survive). Because of this, women have evolved over the millennia to respond to what are called honest signals: evidence of good genes that cannot be faked.

For women, a man's physical fitness, height, and other physical features do trigger sexual attraction because they signal good reproductive health. However, women are much more responsive to <u>behavioral</u> evidence of reproductive value than men because women have to make a much larger investment in their children (9 months vs 2 minutes). As a result, women desire a man who displays honest signals that indicate he would make an effective father (i.e. someone who would help her child thrive).

We evolved in hunter gatherer tribes of 50-150 members, in these tribes, males with high-status had the most power, and therefore, the best genes for a woman to pass on to the next generation (children with high-status fathers would have access to more food and would inherit some of their father's status). Because of this, status evolved to be the most powerful trigger for attraction.

Men normally chase status through fame, money, and possessions, but this is incredibly inefficient because women's brains didn't evolve to respond to Ferrari's or mansions, external status symbols didn't exist in the environment we evolved in. Instead, women evolved to respond to the emotional signals of status, because they couldn't be faked.

High-status behaviors couldn't be faked because if a male who were lowstatus acted confidently (for example, by making an advance on a desirable female), higher status males would see this as a challenge to their authority. At best a low status male who tried to assert himself would be put in his place, at worst he would be ostracized or killed by the leaders of the tribe. To survive, a low status male would have to take what scraps he could get and act as males with authority expected him to (submissively).

Fortunately, in the modern world, acting confidently is a comparatively riskfree behavior. Unfortunately, building confidence is challenging because it requires you to overcome a primal resistance to confident behaviors that evolved to prevent you from getting yourself killed. Confidence is the most powerful honest signal to develop, because if you act confidently you are signaling that you are highstatus, and if you are high-status you have high reproductive value, and high reproductive value automatically triggers attraction.

The Path to Mastery

To cause a woman to feel an emotional desire to sleep with you, you must show her that you are confident. The concept is simple, but implementation is not. By completing the challenges in the following section, you will learn to show women that you are exceptionally confident, and if you make it to the end, you will earn an abundant dating life.

Of course, confidence isn't everything, but a confident attitude when combined with risk taking will net you more results than an infinite number of pick up artist tricks like the annihilation method or the apocalypse opener ever could (and I've tried them all, many times). Besides, pick up techniques can only work if you project extreme confidence, learning them is pointless until you've mastered that underlying fundamental.

With that said, if you complete these challenges, and are disappointed with your results, message me at aghayden@email.arizona.edu explaining your circumstances, and I will provide you with an hour of free weekly skype coaching for four weeks (normally $40/hr). --

Each challenge builds on the last, because of this, you should choose the appropriate starting point based on your current experience level.

If you are a beginner, start with the first challenge.

If you are an intermediate, you may skip challenges 1 and 2.

If you are advanced, you may start with challenge 7 and continue through both bonus challenges.

Do not skip any days or challenges past your starting point. If you take the attitude that it's fine to skip something here or there, it becomes very easy to start on a slippery slope that leads you to veer off the path completely, psychologists have found that simple, unambiguous goals (called bright lines) are the most effective.

Brothers Chip and Dan Heath, authors of the acclaimed book, Switch put it best, "We're all loophole exploiting lawyers when it comes to our own self-control." The challenges are designed to develop consistency, doing some things right some of the time will severely limit your results; instead, each of the weekly challenges allows you to develop a skill and repeat it enough so that it will become habitual and automatic, but to get the results you want, you must have realistic expectations.

You Will Make Excuses

We inevitably start self-improvement journeys wearing rose-colored goggles. We commit to improve ourselves when we are in a motivated state, and it feels like that motivation will last indefinitely. We lose ourselves in excitement and forget that there will be many obstacles that need to be prepared for in advance so they can be overcome.

You will make excuses, and if you don't prepare for them, they will convince you to give up on your pursuit at some point.

The most common type of excuses are called rationalizations. Your brain evolved over millions of years to conserve energy and avoid risk. Approaching women requires a large exertion of willpower, and to your brain, represents a significant risk (if you approached the wrong woman in caveman times you would have been ostracized or even killed). To prevent you from wasting energy and taking risks, your brain will generate negative emotions, you will be flooded with stress and anxiety when you go out. Your mind will formulate seemingly logical explanations for those negative emotions with elaborate rationalizations.

Rationalizations are clever, because they seem to make logical sense.

There is a particularly common rationalizations that men seeking to improve their dating life are often tricked by, because it can make every rejection seem like proof that you aren't good enough for high quality women, but the rationalization is really just an elaborate illusion created by society, and then reinforced by your own perception.

What You See is All There Is

If you haven't had much success with attractive women so far in your life, your brain is going to make sense of this unfortunate fact by generating seemingly logical reasons that explain why you've been unlucky in love.

For some men, these rationalizations will be about their physical appearance (I'm not tall/jacked/handsome enough) and for others they will be about their status (I need to make more money/have a better car).

These rationalizations aren't arbitrary, they reflect widely held cultural values. We are inundated with the idea (from Hollywood, advertisements, and societal stereotypes) that we need to look a certain way, have certain possessions, and be high status to get the women we want. Because of this, it's natural to think you need those things. Thinking that way can lead you to conclude that you shouldn't waste your time and effort in a (futile) attempt to date extremely attractive women.

It gets worse, once you develop the belief that you aren't good enough for certain women, that belief becomes self-reinforcing. Your life is going to keep giving you evidence that you don't deserve particularly attractive women, because there isn't going to be a point in your life when beautiful women miraculously start approaching you and begging to suck your dick. Therefore, each month that goes by in which you don't successfully date an attractive woman, the notion that you're not good enough for one is being reinforced.

This self-fulfilling prophecy becomes even more ruthless because the belief that you don't deserve beautiful women will be reflected in your behavior around them. Your negative beliefs are going to make you uncomfortable around women you're attracted to, which will lead you to act doubtful and anxious in their company. As a result, attractive women will feel uncomfortable around you.

You will notice that attractive women are uncomfortable around you, and that they clearly don't find you attractive. You will conclude (naturally) that these high-quality women don't find you attractive because you lack high-status or traditional good looks; when in reality, they're not attracted to you because of your lack of self-confidence.

It's a truly vicious cycle, our culture reinforces the notion that you need to be physically attractive, have high status, or be wealthy to date beautiful women; so when you don't date beautiful women, you'll think it must be because you lack the attributes society has taught you are necessary. Then you provide yourself with more evidence that you need money, looks, and status because attractive women don't seem to like you, they seem uncomfortable around you. You assume this is because you don't have the external attributes that society deifies, even though it's really because of your uncomfortable behavior.

To escape this cycle, you must get evidence that you are attractive to high quality women. How? By approaching them and reflecting on what you could have done differently (I will show you how soon). By focusing on what you could have done differently in a field report, you're empowering yourself to start to notice the aspects of interactions that are under your control. As you adjust your approach based on these observations, you will notice the responses you get start to improve.

You will start to gather evidence that the most important variable for your ability to attract high quality women is not something outside of your control like your physical appearance or wealth, but your own behavior.

As you progressively push yourself further, you will gradually gather more evidence that your rationalizations are in fact, untrue, and you will free yourself of a mental prison that was created by society but then reinforced by your own mind.

Eight Weeks

In the following section, there are eight challenges each of which will take a minimum of one week to complete. The challenges grow progressively more difficult to ensure that you make steady forward progress. You will be required to go out seven days a week, starting with a requirement of only 15 minutes per day. This is important, dabbling <u>never</u> works, and consistency is essential to habit formation and long-term results.

After you complete a challenge successfully for seven total days, you progress to the next challenge. If on any day, you do not successfully complete your challenge, you will be required to repeat that day. So, if on the fourth day of your challenge you approach two women, but your challenge is to approach five women, your next attempt will count as the fourth day again. You will advance to the fifth day when you successfully approach five women.

It's preferable to track which day you're on for your current challenge, you can track your progress with a simple excel spreadsheet, word document, or productivity app like Todoist.

Each challenge is split into several parts

1: Rules, exactly what you must do to successfully complete the challenge. You will be provided with measurable criteria so that if you complete the challenge, improvement will be inevitable.

2: The concept behind the challenge; why it's important, and how it works.

3. A journal entry about what happened, this is often called a field report.

Those who write quality field reports consistently make significantly faster progress than those who don't, in fact, it's just as important as going out. Most men who read pickup content do not write field reports consistently, and this limits their rate of progress.

Field Reports Catalyze Change

There are two primary reasons why so few guys who follow pickup advice write field reports:

1. It is unclear why they are so essential to making progress.

2. It's difficult to know exactly what to write to make a field report effective.

Once you write good field reports for a week consecutively, it will become clear why they are so powerful. Field reports allow you to learn from your actions in a non-emotional, objective way.

In the moment, rejection can feel like evidence that you are not good enough for attractive women. It can feel humiliating, and sometimes, even emasculating. However, when writing a field report about that rejection later, you can see it for what it really was, and you can interpret what felt like a disempowering memory in an entirely different light.

When you write about what you learned from a rejection, you have the opportunity to realize that your emotional reaction to it was really just an ego trip on your part. With a field report you can transform failures into powerful learning experiences that help you adapt and mature. Each time you catch negative thinking in your field reports, you will become more aware that those negative thoughts aren't real, and therefore will be less affected by them in the future.

These observations will genuinely change how you think, psychologist Robert Cialdini found that the words we write about ourselves can change our identities and behaviors to an uncanny degree (Influence, pg 53), we live our lives absorbed in our own story, by writing effective field reports you can shift from the role of a reader, to that of an author.

Field Report Guidelines

Each challenge will be accompanied with guidelines for what to focus on in that challenge's field reports. These guidelines point out topics and lessons you may want to focus on.

Field Report Examples

For each challenge, you will be provided one to two edited field reports from a previous student of mine. These are especially important, reading them will allow you to understand what elements are included in an effective field report. Use them as guidance for your own reports.

The field report examples also give you a realistic look at what you should expect from each challenge. By going into my student's head, you will see how he learned from failures and roadblocks, many of which you will encounter as well. Handling failure well is a powerful catalyst for success, and these field report examples will give you a unique perspective to learn from that would normally be inaccessible.

Do Whatever It Takes

If you tend to start pursuing your goals with wild enthusiasm, but often quit before you've made meaningful progress, then a website designed by Harvard psychologists may be helpful to you. Stickk.com can force you to take action consistently over a long period of time.

Stickk.com allows you to make a commitment contract for any goal of your choosing, and it provides you with consequences for failing that goal. After you select a goal, you choose a consequence for failure (money is most effective). Select an amount of money you aren't willing to lose, and choose who receives it if you fail (can be a friend, charity, or even anti-charity). Then, select a referee who will determine whether you succeeded in your commitment (this prevents cheating). If you fail your commitment, the stakes will be sent to your chosen recipient.

Any wingman you have should be happy to referee for you (if you don't have any wings, checkout appendix a to learn how to find one).

Section 2: Trial by Fire

Challenge One: Get Your Feet Wet

Rules:

-Go out for 15 minutes each day for a week.

-Must go to a location where attractive women congregate.

Explanation

Sound unnecessarily simple? You would think, yet a silent majority of those who consume dating advice content spend tens or even hundreds of hours accumulating knowledge, but rarely if ever go out. Hell, this was me at one point, I had a burning desire to get this area of my life handled, yet I was terrified of rejection, so I watched hundreds of videos and read numerous books. But did I go out? Only once in my first year. I convinced myself I was making progress, just like so many guys I've met who spend most of their time on the sidelines, only going out on rare occasion.

It is very easy to convince yourself that reading books and watching videos is a suitable substitute to taking real action. You will tell yourself you're not ready to go out yet, that you need to learn the ropes first. This satiates your desire to feel like you're making progress towards your goal, while also allowing you to avoid taking any real risk. But if you do this, you won't make any progress.

You might think you wouldn't fall into this trap, but the cleverness in this line of thinking, is that you won't know you're doing it. Any emotions or thoughts that try to convince you to procrastinate are actually rationalizations disguised as good logic.

If you feel emotional resistance to going out, but go out anyway, you prove to your mind that nothing bad will happen if you go out, that the risk isn't as real as you felt it was. The next time you face that risk, your emotional resistance won't be as strong, until eventually, your resistance will vanish completely. In short, the only way out, is through.

Challenge one is an opportunity to shock your system to catalyze change. Your first challenge is to go out every day for fifteen minutes to an area where you can meet attractive women. Nothing more is required of you. This may seem too easy, but it is important to make progress gradually. Approaching women can be a big leap, if it were easy, you would already be doing it regularly.

This challenge is designed so you don't overwhelm yourself, if you take an action that is too challenging for your skill level, it creates anxiety. Being in an environment with a high density of people can be anxiety provoking on its own, but not so anxiety provoking that you will trigger insurmountable resistance.

Even if this challenge seems too easy for you, keep in mind that you are required to go out seven days in a row, and to make a habit of writing a field report each time you go out. Also, know that you are not in any way limited by the challenge, you can and should do more than the minimum if you can. If you can approach twenty women, do it. The purpose of challenge 1 is to get you to start building a habit of going out in a sustainable way, it is designed to account for an important but neglected concept from the psychology of motivation, want-to versus have-to motivation.

Have-to motivation is the fuel that wakes us up at 7:30 am to get ready for our 9-5, it's what makes us do what to our boss tells us to even when we disagree with them; have-to motivation compels us to do the dishes, read textbooks, and go to jury duty. Have-to motivation is important, but it has significant limitations. Doing something because of have-to motivation is stressful and often thoroughly unenjoyable. When have-to motivation is used to complete self-improvement goals, it doesn't work.

If going out to meet women is consistently stressful, you will eventually burn out. Unfortunately, when we make self-improvement goals they tend to be too rigorous and, as a result, rely on have-to motivation. For example, if your goal were to approach three girls each day, but you have never approached a girl before, you will experience significant psychological tension while you are out, and that unrealistic self-expectation will flood your body with negative emotions and their associated rationalizations. Those emotions and rationalizations are not a valid excuse, but at the same time, it's better to make the process of growth as enjoyable as possible, because the more fun you have going out and talking to women, the more addictive and self-sustaining the habit will become. You want to be hard on yourself, but not too hard, it's a delicate balance, but if you get it right, your rate of progress will be exponentially faster than if you force yourself to endure extraordinary distress.

Want-to motivation, on the other hand, is the fuel that compels us to eat Cheetos and watch porn, it motivates us to take actions that are intrinsically enjoyable, and want-to-motivation, unsurprisingly, makes progress and goal completion significantly easier and more sustainable.

By setting realistic expectations, you are giving yourself the opportunity to rely on less have-to motivation and more want-to motivation. If your baseline for success is high enough to make progress, but not so high that it is too stressful, you are more likely to enter a flow state in which your performance and enjoyment will be exponentially increased. If you have reasonable expectations of yourself, you might find yourself inspired to exceed those expectations because you want to, and in so doing, making progress will be enjoyable for its own sake.

Venues

There are several good venue options. Clubs and bars are best at night, and college campuses and malls are best in the day. If you work in the morning, you can go to the mall for fifteen minutes before you go home, or you can go out at night for fifteen minutes at 12:00 a.m. and take a nap in the evening beforehand if you want more sleep. Seriously, don't bullshit yourself, unless you work over 100 hours per week, you have plenty of time, and if you must adjust your sleep schedule, don't hesitate to do so.

If you live in a town that is too small to have a decent option for nightlife every day of the night, then go either to your local college campus, a mall, or a busy street during the day and do your approaches then. If that's not an option, go to the area in your city with the most bars or clubs, and go out, even if there's only five people in each bar, that's still enough to make a lot of progress. And although it might feel awkward or stupid at first, you may end up surprised by the results you can get even when so few people are out.

Field Report Guidelines

As soon as you get home, start writing your field report. This will give you the opportunity to analyze what happened objectively since you will have some emotional distance, and to reinterpret what happened in a more logical, and therefore beneficial, way.

It's completely normal to have negative, self-defeating thoughts and feelings when you go out. Field reports allow you to notice them for what they are, just thoughts and feelings, not external reality. For example, if you notice you were anxious, you can use your field report to interpret why you were anxious, to help prove to yourself that the anxiety was made up in your mind. You might write in your field report: "I saw a beautiful girl walking between classes, but I saw that she was looking at her phone, and I thought she wouldn't want to talk to me, that she was too busy. But if I think about it, I don't know that she would be annoyed, the only way to find out would be to go talk to her. And even if she was mildly annoyed by my approach? So what? Why was I so nervous over something that wouldn't really matter?"

At the same time, if you do anything above your expectations, write it down as well, "I felt nervous and hesitant, but I saw this girl standing by the bar, and I introduced myself. It didn't go anywhere, but it was exhilarating to face my fear."

When you write about the fact that you did something you didn't think you would be able to do, you are reminding yourself that your limiting beliefs aren't true, because if they were, you wouldn't be able to exceed your own expectations.

This reminder serves as powerful motivational fuel to keep going, surpassing a limit you thought you had is one of the most empowering experiences you can have, and this is an experience you will have frequently if you complete these challenges.

If while you walk around a venue, you have thoughts about people judging you, write those down as well, "I thought people were staring at me, that they were judging me as weird or creepy. I have no idea why I would have thought that, I know they don't really care about what I was doing on an intellectual level, but it felt so real that I bought into it, and I found myself getting anxious as a result."

As you write and interpret these thoughts and feelings, you will realize they are totally absurd, even though they feel real. This is a good thing, everyone has these thoughts, but few people become aware of them, which is the key to letting go of them.

Make sure to include what you did, what you hesitated to do, how you felt, and why you felt that way. If you don't know what that should look like, make sure to look over the sample field report immediately before you write your own for guidance.

Example Field Report: Challenge 1 Day 1

What I did and why:

I went to the club alone at about 11:00. I felt a knot in my stomach on the way, I was nervous just from the thought of approaching women, even though I knew I didn't have to yet. As soon as I got into the club I felt anxious and had a strong desire to leave. I felt like it was pointless to be there, and that I wouldn't really make any progress. Yet, I persisted because I knew I really wanted to improve my dating life, and I was already at the club, so I figured I might as well finish the challenge.

I wandered around the club, and considered approaching a few girls, but each time I did so, I hesitated. I noticed each time I hesitated I felt pissed off at myself, probably because I was paralyzed by anxiety even though I knew there was nothing to be afraid of. After the fifteen minutes were up, I felt fairly stressed, but at the same time I felt proud of myself because I had taken the first leap of faith I needed to take to start changing who I am, and although I didn't get laid, I started to face my fears.

Example Field Report: Level 1 Day 7

What I did and why:

At this point, going to the club was much less anxiety provoking, however I still found that a lot of the girls at the club were intimidating, and I still felt nervous when I saw girls I wanted to talk to, and I kept making excuses like, "She's with friends, she probably has a boyfriend." However, I was happy that it was getting easier to go out.

I still put pressure on myself to actually do approaches, and this made me a bit nervous. Surprisingly, a girl approached me, and asked why I was at the club alone. I lied to her, and said I was waiting for a friend (because I was embarrassed).

We talked for a few minutes before she walked away, she was surprisingly friendly.

Afterwards, I almost gathered up the courage to walk up to a girl, but I couldn't think of something to say, so I changed my mind. Throughout the night, there were still a bunch of negative thoughts going through my mind, I told myself I wasn't good looking enough, I wasn't funny enough, I was too awkward, and that girls would make fun of me if I talked to them. I even had thoughts of security dragging me out if I dared talk to a girl. I am getting to be a bit more aware of my negative thoughts, but they still have a strong emotional effect on me, and I still believe them more than I should. However, progress is always good, and this week I made a lot of progress. Especially considering its been over a year since I've been on a date.

Note: If you are unsure if your field report is effective, or if you have any questions about your field reports, email me at aghayden@email.arizona.edu and I will provide you with personal feedback, free of charge.

Do This if You're Having Trouble

Level 2 will have you approaching strangers, if you haven't done this before, it can be a big leap. Remember that you want to push yourself, but not too hard. If you find yourself attempting challenge two but failing multiple times, I recommend finding a wingman (how to do so is covered in appendix a). Make a deal with your wing, give them $100 cash (or whatever amount is enough to motivate you), and tell them that you get $20 back for each approach you do. This might be stressful, but it will get you to take that first step, do this as many times as necessary until you can approach without money on the line.

This strategy applies to any challenge in which you hit a roadblock, it's good to be enthusiastic, but it's necessary to be prepared for setbacks you may encounter. You likely will be able to complete each challenge on your own, but don't hesitate to use external resources.

Challenge 2: Open

Rules:

(30 minutes min)- The minimum time limit means that even if you complete the challenge in less than that amount of time, to count the day as a success you must stay out for at least this amount of time.

-Each day, ask at least 1 woman for directions.

Examples:

1. "Hi, do you know where somewhere good to eat is nearby?"

2. "Hi, do you know of any other good clubs nearby?"

-Whenever you feel able to, replace asking for directions with the following:

"Hi, I'm (your name), I saw you and I wanted to introduce myself."
Explanation:

This challenge may be exceptionally difficult if you are new to pickup, but it also has the potential to be especially thrilling.

Approaching strangers takes a lot of courage (remember, your brain unconsciously thinks strangers represent mortal danger). The only way to disprove this unconscious fear and free yourself from your anxiety is to face it directly. Every time you talk to a stranger, you are giving your brain evidence that strangers don't represent any real, physical danger, and over time, this will lead you to feel less anxiety around other people.

Asking for directions gives you plausible deniability, it's easier to ask for directions than to tell a girl you find her attractive directly because there's less risk of rejection. Once you are comfortable asking for directions, you can transition to introducing yourself directly.

To complete the challenge, you must introduce yourself directly at least once during the week, if you've only asked for directions, you cannot move on to the next week.

After you've introduced yourself, you can say, "How's it going today?" To keep the conversation going, if the conversation dies out, that's fine, it might feel awkward, but afterward you'll realize it wasn't a big deal.

Field Report Guidelines

Make sure to write about how you felt before an approach. Did you hesitate? What did you think would happen? Pick apart the logic of any thoughts you had, if you thought you were going to interrupt her, ask yourself why that's such a bad thing. If you thought she wouldn't like you, why did you think that? If you think you do have reason to believe she wouldn't have liked you, why does it matter whether she did?

Starting this week, write a short section about whether you were having fun.

Ask yourself what your agenda was when talking to girls, were you interacting with them to improve their day, or were you trying to get something? Did you need the girl to like you to feel okay about yourself? If so, why?

Example Field Report Challenge 2 Day 1

What did I do? Why?

I went to the local university campus, and I felt extremely anxious on the way there. I tried to figure out what I feared, but I couldn't figure it out. I knew that my anxiety was a sign that I needed to do this, and I knew I would have to face my fears to be free of them. I walked towards the campus and saw some girls who I could have approached, but I told myself I should wait until I got to the food court, and then I would approach girls. (Which made no sense obviously). When I arrived at the food court, I decided I needed to get some water first, then water turned to lunch. As I sat there, eating, I saw some girls I found intriguing, and I knew I should have talked to them. I told myself I should wait to finish eating and that it was weird for me to approach girls here because I go to the local community college, not the university, and I would get caught as an outsider who was trying to hit on girls. Looking back at it, I doubt anyone would really care, and even if they did, so what? But the only way to find out if my fears are true or not is to face them, if I don't, they will keep causing me anxiety and stress.

When I finished my meal, I felt even more anxious, probably because I hadn't taken any action yet. I kept thinking that I was a creep to want to talk to girls, and I felt a weird feeling of shame for what I was doing. I really wonder where that comes from, because obviously, talking to girls you find attractive is one of the most natural things in the world, so why would I feel a sense of shame for doing so?

I walked around campus and I noticed myself making excuses for why I shouldn't talk to each girl I saw. One girl was busy reading, another was looking at her phone, a third girl was too attractive for me. Looking back, these excuses obviously didn't make any sense, but they felt real in the moment. These excuses were rationalizations, I felt anxious to talk to strangers because I was afraid of rejection, and to make that fear seem reasonable, my mind came up with seemingly logical excuses.

After about 30 minutes of walking around, I felt something come over me, a weird surge of motivation. I walked up to a girl who was sitting down looking at her phone and I asked, "Where is the nearest Burger King?" She said, "In the food court." I said thanks, and I walked away in a rush, I literally wanted to run. I felt extremely nervous, my heart was pumping, my legs were shaking. I started telling myself I needed to go to Burger King in case she checked if I was there. I have no idea why I thought that, it was a very neurotic thought. As my nerves cooled down, I started to feel excited about approaching women for the first time. I felt a huge weight lift off my shoulders, I had just taken a big step in the right direction, and the girl was really nice.

I felt extremely enthusiastic at this point, and so I decided to let myself off the hook by going home. I felt so proud of myself that I wanted to leave on a high note, looking back I think I should have kept going. Perhaps the biggest lesson I learned today was that taking a leap of faith and talking to a stranger felt good, not because it went well, but because I faced my fear. I'm still nervous about the rest of these challenges, but some of my fear is turning into excitement, and I'm starting to believe I will really make progress if I keep at it.

Example Field Report Challenge 2 Day 7

So, I skipped a day, meaning this is really the 8th day since I started challenge 2. I skipped day 6 because even though I was making progress and starting to enjoy myself at times, I also felt stressed about facing my anxieties, and told myself I deserved a break. I was tempted to take another day off, but I caught myself. I knew I was just rationalizing an excuse to avoid changing myself, and so I decided to go out again today.

I still felt a decent amount of nerves going out, but noticeably less than the first day. I still hesitated quite a few times on my walk towards campus. I told myself, "Not yet." Whenever I saw a girl who caught my eye. Honestly, that didn't even make sense, it was a bad excuse looking back at it. I also noticed I was anxious about running into a girl I saw before, and getting 'caught'. I thought that she would accuse me of being a creep or something. I was also afraid of getting a reputation and becoming known as the guy who asks girls for directions to burger king, so I decided to ask for directions to another restaurant.

I kept thinking that I was wasting my time, and that I should just meet some girl on Plenty of Fish, or that I should put this off until I had a better job or got in better shape. I kept thinking this as I walked around looking for girls to approach.

After about 10 minutes, I saw a girl sitting down and I sucked it in, I asked her for directions to Taco Bell. She said she didn't know and that I should use my GPS. I felt extremely anxious when she said this, and I apologized for asking before walking away. I felt judged and rejected. I felt like this meant I wasn't good enough, and I wanted to walk home. I made such a big deal out of this reaction, but now, looking back, I think it was silly, it really wasn't a big deal, but I made it one. This just shows that I have to learn to get over myself, and not make such a big deal of what people think, there's no reason to care so much.

I kept going because I didn't want to have to do this challenge another day if I didn't do part two of the challenge by introducing myself directly. I walked up to another girl sitting down to ask for directions, and even though I was very nervous, she was much nicer than the first girl. I did this a couple more times, and I almost started to look forward to approaching girls after the fourth approach. The fourth girl I talked to was also especially nice, and I think it might have been because I was in a positive mood.

Afterwards, I decided it was time to directly introduce myself to a girl. I felt very nervous and hesitant, as if this were a really big deal, but I sucked it in. I walked up to a girl who was on her laptop and said, "Hi I'm Kevin." She said hi and told me her name and we shook hands. There was an awkward pause before I said, "How's your day going." She said it was good and asked me the same back. I asked her what her major was and she told me it was Journalism. The whole time I was literally shaking from my nervousness. I told her that her major sounded cool, and walked away, before going home with a mixture of frustration and excitement.

The Devil's Nectar

Alcohol is a crutch, it lowers your social inhibitions which makes you more confident, and therefore, more likely to get immediate results. This can lead you take actions that would normally be outside of your comfort zone.

However, there are consequences to getting drunk when you go out. Alcohol limits your ability to learn, and your field reports won't be nearly as valuable when you drink (because your memory will be hazy).

If you rely on alcohol as a crutch, you will associate drinking with meeting girls. You might be a confident risk taker drunk, but it won't translate to your sober state much.

Having a couple drinks isn't damaging, but if you are getting wasted, alcohol will do more harm than good in the long term. Be honest with yourself, if you can't limit yourself to a couple drinks, you should avoid alcohol entirely.

Challenge Three: Just Two Minutes

Rules:

(minimum 45 minutes)

-Begin interactions with "Hi, I'm (your name), I saw you and I wanted to introduce myself."

-You may also use a more direct approach and say, "Hey, I thought you were cute and I had to say hi."

-Each day, you must engage in one conversation that lasts for at least two minutes.

(You can estimate the time, but it would be preferable to use a stopwatch or timer.)

-Each day at home. Practice the provided free association exercise for at least 5 minutes.

Exercise:

Complete a sentence out-loud, then create a new and unrelated sentence using a word from the previous sentence. (You can do this in writing if you prefer) Example:

1. The universe has existed for billions of <u>years.</u>

2. I am 25 <u>years</u> old today, that's half way to fifty.

3. Half of <u>marriages</u> end in divorce.

4. <u>Marriage</u> is known to be a cultural universal, which is weird because I heard that monogamy wasn't natural.

Make sure not to tell a story, if you do, the exercise won't be building your free association skills. Each sentence must use a word from the previous sentence, but in a new context, not to continue the previous thought.

Explanation

Striking up a conversation with a stranger can be anxiety provoking, keeping it going can seem even more difficult. Small talk like, "Nice weather, eh?" or, "Did you see the game?", usually goes nowhere. So, how can you keep the conversation going?

If you were to analyze a good conversation you had with a friend, you would notice it was not a logical exchange of information, but something more like a free-association exercise.

Practicing the provided exercise will help you to make these kinds of creative connections naturally in all of your conversations. Not only will you be more engaging in conversations with women you meet, but more engaging in general.

Do not force yourself to free associate in conversations, as you practice this exercise you will start to do so automatically. Trying to force this is like trying to be funny on command, it's ineffective, and can even be awkward.

If you are in a conversation but you are not naturally free associating, it's okay to use a crutch to keep the conversation going. Memorize these basic questions so that you can maintain a conversation even if you can't think of anything to say:

What do you do?

Are you from here?

What are you up to today?

What are you passionate about?

The conversation derived from questions like these isn't ideal, but it's useful to have a contingency plan if you're in your head and can't think of anything especially clever or interesting to say.

Based on her responses to your questions you can ask her further questions to expand the conversation, and you may find commonalities which can lead to a much deeper conversation and a sense of connection between the two of you.

For example, if she's going to school to be a therapist and you read psychology/self-help books in your free time you can go deep into the subject.

Interview questions aren't as engaging as free association, but they can be a good way to get to know each other and vibe on commonalities.

At first this challenge may be uncomfortable, and you might feel like you have nothing to say. But each day that you push yourself through this, talking to strangers will become more natural until you get to the point where having engaging and meaningful conversations with people you've just met becomes effortless.

Field Report Guidelines

For this challenge, you're going to be putting your ego on the line, and you might get some negative reactions or rejections. Some girls won't want to talk to you. This can easily send you on an ego-trip if you let your emotions take over. Write about any approaches in which you felt upset or hurt. Write about why it affected you so much, and pick it apart to see if it's really as big a deal as you think it is. For example, if you got rejected, ask yourself, whether it meant that you are inherently flawed, or if you could have done anything differently. If you thought the approach was perfect, but she didn't like you, is it worth taking it personally? Or is it natural that not everyone will like you?

Find the humor in each approach. Realize the if you got butthurt it's actually pretty funny that you would take yourself so seriously. Each time you find the humor in emotional pain, you'll free yourself from a little bit more of your ego.

Don't hesitate to give yourself props. Very few people will build up the courage to talk to strangers like you have, that's something to be proud of even if you didn't get the reactions you wanted.

Challenge Three Day 1

Today, I wasn't nervous to go out, I was actually pretty excited. I went to a busy college bar. While I was waiting in line looking at the people around me, I started to overanalyze, and then my anxiety came back. I thought they were looking at me and judging me. I felt concerned about the challenge, even though I had already approached a good number of women last week. I also felt impatient, like I should be going on dates by now, but I remembered that if I wanted to ask girls on dates, there was nothing stopping me from going for it.

When I entered the bar, I did my routine to procrastinate approaching women. I got some water, walked around the bar, and got some more water, telling myself I would approach after I had finished the routine. Afterwards, I meandered around the club somewhat uncomfortably.

I still found the women in the club intimidating, and I looked for a girl who wasn't particularly physically attractive to talk to, because I felt that it wouldn't hurt as much if a girl who I didn't find attractive were to reject me. I also told myself that this was a good way to warm up for the girls who I found more intimidating. I felt that if I started by approaching an attractive girl, I would waste my time with her, and that I needed to 'get in the zone', before doing so. That might be true on some level, but there's plenty of attractive women, and even if I approach one and its awkward, I can always approach them a second time later in the night when I'm in a better state.

I found a girl who didn't intimidate me and introduced myself. I immediately started asking the questions I had memorized. The conversation wasn't particularly interesting, but we kept talking for a few minutes, and I even made her laugh a couple times. I got the sense that she was attracted to me. I wanted to stay in the conversation even though I wasn't attracted to the girl, I was genuinely enjoying myself. Her friends eventually pulled her way to 'go to the bathroom', looking back, I'm really happy with how this went.

I walked up to another girl who was a bit more intimidating. She told me she had a boyfriend right off the bat. I responded by saying I had a boyfriend as well. She smiled, but then it got awkwardly quiet, I decided to push through and I asked where she was from. She told me she had to go find her friends. I was really frustrated by this response. I felt a strange resentment towards her, even though I knew she had a boyfriend and that ending the conversation with me wasn't a personal insult. This killed my mood for a while, I started to get wrapped up in negative thoughts. I told myself attractive girls didn't like me, that I wasn't good looking enough, that I should just give up. Just from one mild rejection, I made such a big deal about this, and honestly, it's kind of funny that I would take it so seriously in hindsight.

I realized I had already been at the bar for 45 minutes, but I decided to stay longer even though I was in a bad mood. I knew that if I pushed through the pain, it would be good for me. I walked up to an attractive girl who was sitting next to a friend and introduced myself. She was very receptive, the conversation flowed naturally. After a few minutes, I felt nervous and then I excused myself. I think she wanted me to ask her to dance or get her number, but I hesitated because I wasn't prepared for this good of a result, and I was afraid she might say no if I asked (which would be a big deal to my fragile ego lol). After this approach, I decided to go back home.

Even though I was frustrated after being rejected, I also had a lot of fun, and had a good conversation with an attractive and interesting girl who seemed to genuinely like me, which makes me think I really will reach my goals if I keep going out consistently and pushing myself.

(From this point forward there will only be one example field report for each level.)

Social Momentum Manifesto

Your first approach of the day will almost always be thrilling. It's like jumping off a high-dive. After that first leap, each subsequent approach becomes less challenging.

Social momentum is a powerful phenomenon that is important to be aware of. When you arrive at a venue, it may feel like the entire night will be anxiety provoking, but as soon as you take that first leap, the anxiety will begin to dissipate. The more you learn to trust in this fact, the easier it will become to approach despite any emotional resistance you feel.

Your first approach will not only reduce the weight of anxiety on your shoulders, but it will build momentum by causing what is known as psychological inertia to work in your favor. In physics, inertia is the law that objects at rest stay at rest, and objects in motion stay in motion. In psychology, inertia is a phenomenon of decision making, it is the reason that starting an exercise routine is often more difficult than finishing a routine you've already begun. Once you approach a woman, your mind lets go of its resistance to taking action and each subsequent approach requires less effort because psychological inertia starts to work in your favor.

There are three steps to building social momentum:

1. Don't discriminate: In any particular environment, only a small percentage of women will be attractive to you. If you only approach these women, you will only have a few 'opportunities' on any given night, and you will only spend a

slim segment of your night actually interacting with women. Instead, approach everyone in the environment, and with most women, just flirt to have fun, when you meet one you like, flirt with real intent. If you have trouble interacting with women you don't find sexually attractive, it signals that you are taking value, that you're trying to get something. If you can have fun with women that you don't want to 'take' sex from, you are coming from a place of offering value, and when you do this, all women will find you more attractive, not just sexually, but socially.

2. Don't hesitate: At the end of each interaction, approach someone else immediately. If as a habit, you return to your group of friends after approaching, break that habit. Time spent between interactions allows your momentum to depreciate, but if you do consecutive approaches with no hesitation in between, you will find yourself getting out of your head and into your body, into a flow state in which your normal limitations don't apply.

3. Escalate: As you take action, make sure to push yourself further over time. If at first you just introduce yourself, in future interactions you can initiate physicality, or ask women for their phone numbers. It would be a good idea to strategize how you intend to push yourself further as the night goes on, for example you could write:

    a. When I arrive at the venue: I will approach women indirectly, and ask how their night is going.

    b. After I am comfortable with indirect approaches, I will approach women more directly, by saying, "I liked your style, and I had to say hi."

c. After I am comfortable with this, I will attempt to lead each interaction forward by asking the girl I am talking to if she would like to dance.

Even if you are new to cold approaching women, using social momentum, you can potentially take actions that are far outside of your usual comfort zone, and potentially even get results that normally only someone with much more experience would be able to get.

Date Field Reports

Starting this week, you're going to be getting phone numbers. This also means you'll start going on dates. Writing field reports for dates is just as useful as for going out, so don't hesitate to do so.

For date field reports, analyze whether you lead the interaction. If you are sitting at a coffee shop for two hours, you're not moving the date forward enough.

Ask yourself how you could have moved it forward, could you have gone on a walk?

Should you have invited her to watch a movie? Why did you hesitate to do so?

Write about whether you connected on an emotional level. Was the conversation awkward? If it was awkward, why? What were you nervous about?

What could you have done differently?

Ask yourself what the vibe was like, were you talking to her like she was a friend, or was there sexuality in the interaction? What was your eye contact like?

Were you physical? If not, why not? Were you judging her at any point? If so, why? In what ways were you offering value? In what ways were you trying to get something from her?

Each time you write a field report for a date, you'll be able to correct course for future dates so that they will be a more enjoyable experience for all involved.

Challenge 4: Digits

Rules:

(1 hour)

-You must approach at least three women each day.

-You must ask at least 1 woman for her phone number.

-To ask for a girl's number you can use the following line, "Hey, you seem cool, we should get coffee sometime. What's your number?"

-Continue practicing your free association exercise each day for five minutes.

Explanation

I remember how hard my heart was beating the first time I asked for a girl's number in high school (during senior year), I was surprised by how unimportant it seemed to be for her; for me this was a big moment.

Asking for a girl's number can feel like a big deal. It really isn't, many girls will give you their number even if they don't have any attention to hang out with you
later.

However, asking for numbers is a skill you need to get comfortable with. Some of your numbers will lead to dates, and dates are a great way to make deeper connections with women (and maybe even have sex) Even if you don't have a romantic spark with a girl you go on a date with, you may find yourself making a new friend.

Even if you are socially awkward, if you ask enough women out, one of them will like you. This week is an opportunity to get some real results if you push yourself hard enough. If you get one girl's number, don't hesitate to keep going, the momentum from the first success will make the next one easier.

What to do with your numbers

'Text game' is mostly a waste of time. You may be able to convince a woman meet you with your witty text banter in some instances: but in the vast majority of cases, if a girl wants to meet you, she will make herself available. All you have to do is suggest a date, time, and place.

The best strategy is to make plans when you get her number. For example:

You: We should hang out some time. When are you free this week?

Her: I'm free Friday evening.

You: Let's get coffee at Epic Cafe on Friday evening.

Her: Okay.

You: What's your number?

When you ask her number, it should be specifically so that you can meet her again later. Once you have her number text her something simple and straight to the point, for example:

Hi (her name) ⏃, it was great meeting you today.

Then, on the day you made plans with her, confirm those plans a couple hours in advance:

"Hey (her name), are we still on for coffee tonight at 8?"

If you have a girl's number but you haven't made plans. After you send an introductory text, message her the following, "When are you free this week?"

If she wants to hang out with you, she will tell you when she's free. If not, she will write that she is busy. If she is genuinely busy, but she does want to hang out with you, she will suggest another time in the future.

For the most part, anything more complicated and intricate is a waste of your time. You're rarely going to make a girl want to hang out with you because of your texts.

Field Report Guidelines

In this week's field report, you're going to record how many numbers you asked for each day. The purpose of this is to be able to compete against yourself and to be able to look at the trend. Peter Drucker said, "What gets measured, improves", this week's field report was designed with that in mind.

Be aware of any hesitation you might have felt for asking a girl for her phone number. Did you feel nervous to ask? Why? What were you thinking about? What was the worst-case scenario? Were those thoughts worth taking seriously?

Example Field Report Challenge 4 Day 1

How many numbers did I ask for? 2

What did I do and why?

Today I felt comfortable walking to campus with the express purpose of talking to women. I've gone out enough days in a row that it feels like a habit, I'm even starting to feel a pull to go out, I really look forward to it.

I did start to feel nerves again as I walked towards the first girl I was going to approach. I decided to use the line "I thought you were cute and I had to say hi," but as I walked towards her, I noticed she was on a facetime call, I then hesitated and walked away. After this, I felt a bit discouraged, and I wandered around for a while before approaching another girl because I wasn't able to find what I did funny. I was taking myself far too seriously. I snapped out of my hesitation faster than usual, and I walked up to a girl I saw. She was walking, and I still am a bit nervous approaching girls that are walking. For some reason, I feel that it's more intrusive (although I know it's really not). I walked up to her and said I thought she was cute. She smiled and said thanks, but told me she was sorry but she had a boyfriend.

I wasn't affected negatively by this rejection, I've gotten used to it, and she wasn't being mean, just honest. More than anything, I felt proud of myself for stepping outside of my comfort zone.

After the quick rejection, I immediately walked towards the next girl that caught my eye, and I told her I thought she was cute and I had to introduce myself.

She responded very positively, and started asking me questions. As we were talking, I was thinking about how I should be asking for her number. There was natural chemistry between us. I decided to take the leap and ask for her number because I knew I would be proud of myself if I did. I told her we should get coffee on Friday at a coffee shop downtown, she agreed, and so we exchanged numbers. After I said goodbye, my heart was racing, my hands were sweating, and I felt on top of the world. It was like a hit from a drug, the hard work was starting to translate into real results, and I felt good about myself in a way I never had before.

After I walked away from her, I considered taking a break to grab some lunch, but I was having fun, and I knew I might as well keep going to see what might happen. I saw a girl who I found attractive nearby and walked up to her to tell her I thought she was cute.

She didn't respond quite as positively as the last girl, but she was still nice. With her, I had to lead the conversation, the free association exercise was paying off because I did a good job at going over a bunch of topics. I didn't think she was particularly attracted to me, but I decided I may as well go for it, so I asked if she'd like to grab coffee on Saturday. She said she had a boyfriend, I responded, "Well, you can still have friends, right?" She said she could, and so I proceeded to get her number.

I was genuinely surprised at myself for being so assertive, I'm starting to notice some real changes in myself. The more risks I take, the more risk taking starts to feel natural. Afterwards, I walked back to my car, feeling great.

Navigating Group Dynamics

You will rarely find attractive women by themselves in clubs and bars. Understanding group dynamics will help you get a woman's friends on your team whereas they may otherwise be an obstacle.

Two Women:

If you have a wingman, this is the ideal situation, you can each focus on one girl, and the four of you can have a good time.

If, however, you are on your own, this group dynamic requires finesse. Engage both women, if you ignore one, she will most likely grow impatient and drag her friend away with her. Flirt with both women, but flirt with the woman you are interested in with genuine intent, and flirt with her friend the way you would flirt with an old lady; just for the fun of it.

If you want something to happen that night, your best chance is to befriend both women. In some cases, the friend will be on your team and make it easy for you to leave with the girl you like. In other cases, your best option will be to leave with both girls when the club closes. At some point, they must separate from each other, and if the girl you're talking with wants to hook up with you, she will have no problem staying with you until her friend leaves. Then, the two of you can make something happen.

Large group of friends

Introduce yourself directly to the girl you're interested in, but make sure to introduce yourself to her friends as well, and to be positive and friendly towards them. Since there are so many friends, it shouldn't be difficult to ask the girl you like to the dance floor, or to get drink just between the two of you.

When she's with a man:

If a woman is with a man, introduce yourself to her first. Ask her how she knows the guy, if she says they just met, ignore him, act like he doesn't exist. If she says he's her friend, befriend him. If she says he's her boyfriend, you can say, "I can tell you're lying," in a flirtatious tone, and judging by her response, you can decide whether they're really together, or if she just doesn't trust you yet. If she's lying you can proceed. If they really are a couple, your efforts would be better spent elsewhere. Like with a group of two girls, your best chance to hook up with her that night is to go with them when the club closes, they have to split up at some point.

Challenge 5: Laser Eyes

Rules:

(1 hr minimum)

-Ask at least two women for their phone numbers.

-Continue your free-association exercise, but now practice in front of a mirror and practice maintaining steady eye contact (with your reflection) as you practice the free-association exercise. (If I were doing this five years ago, I would have felt extremely embarrassed at the thought of this exercise, but if you feel embarrassed it's an opportunity to take yourself less seriously and get more comfortable in your own skin.)

-While out, look at attractive women you see in the eyes (with a slight smile). If they look back, hold eye contact until after they break it. If they don't meet your gaze, look away after about 3 seconds.

-In each interaction, be aware of your eye contact.

Explanation

Eye contact is one of the most powerful indicators of your confidence level. Making strong, comfortable eye contact acts as an honest signal that you are someone with high self-confidence.

Eye contact can trigger attraction on its own. Famed evolutionary psychologist David Buss writes in his book, Why Women Have Sex,

"In one study, forty-eight women and men came to a lab and were asked to stare into each other's eyes while talking. The effect of mutual gaze proved powerful. Many reported that deep eye contact with an opposite-sex stranger created feelings of intense love. Another study had strangers first reveal intimate details of their lives to each other for half an hour, and then asked them to stare into each other's eyes for four minutes— without breaking eye contact or making any conversation. Participants again reported deep attraction to their study partners. Two of these total strangers even ended up getting married!"

Eye contact is the single most powerful form of nonverbal communication. And unlike body language or vocal projection, eye contact can be easily learned. At first, making stronger eye contact may feel uncomfortable, but after some practice it will feel natural, and it will have an intoxicating effect on those you interact with.

By practicing making eye contact while speaking on your own time at home, your eye contact will improve when interacting with women without needing to make any conscious effort. However, you should still be consciously aware of how you eye contact is in your interactions so that you can learn from your observations.

Intentionally holding eye contact with women you meet when you go out without breaking it first helps you build a habit of making strong eye contact.

For this week, your goal is to ask two women for their number each day, it is important to keep pushing yourself further each week so that you don't get stuck on a plateau for longer than necessary.

Field Report Guidelines

Focus on your eye contact without neglecting other elements of your day or night out. Was your eye contact strong or weak? Did you feel nervous making eye contact, or powerful? What emotions were your eyes projecting? How was your eye contact making the women you met feel? Was your eye contact too aggressive and intimidating? Did you notice your attraction or positive emotions towards women you interacted with increase as you made strong eye contact?

Example Field Report Challenge 5 Day 1

How many numbers did I ask for? 3

What did I do and why?

Ladies night was packed as usual. As I waited in line, I realized that there was no reason to wait until I got in the club to start talking to people. There was a group of three girls behind me and I asked if they were ready to get turnt (lol), they responded enthusiastically and we chatted a bit. As I got inside, I approached the first girl I saw. Her response was neutral at first, but as I focused on my eye contact, I noticed myself getting more attracted to her, and it seemed she got more attracted to me as well. I noticed I was a little nervous making strong eye contact, but it gave the interaction a lot of charge. I suggested we get coffee out of habit, she said it sounded like a good idea, and I got her number.

I walked around the club looking for a particularly attractive girl, as I did so, I made a point to make eye contact with women and to hold it for a few seconds.

When girls locked eyes with me I felt a lot pressure and I looked away before they did a few times.

I noticed as I walked around, my mood started to worsen. I knew it would be better to just talk to someone rather than wander around aimlessly, so I approached the next girl I saw. She liked me, and I got her number as well. I considered asking her to dance, but I decided that this wasn't part of my challenge yet, so I didn't do it.

Looking back, that was a lame rationalization, and I should have just asked her to dance.

After a couple more approaches, I got in the zone. I wasn't thinking much, I was just taking action, and the interactions were going well. I made stronger eye contact than usual, and for the most part it seemed to get positive reactions. It was a bit nerve-wracking to make strong eye contact, but girls didn't give me weird looks or anything like I worried they might.

One girl I approached was very standoffish, I told her I wasn't hitting on her, I just was a social guy, she started acting nicer after this. But her boyfriend came in and tried to intimidate me. It kind of worked, I felt uncomfortable, and after the interaction I noticed I was feeling somewhat bitter.

As the night went on, my state started to dip and I started feel upset that I wasn't in a flow state anymore. I felt like I deserved to be in the zone, and that's probably why I lost it, I was taking myself too seriously again.

I went home after about two hours, even though my mood dipped towards the end, I felt good about myself. I know I've made tremendous progress in these last few weeks, and I know that change is really possible. Going out is getting less anxiety provoking and more fun over time, and when I get I a flow state like tonight, it's about the best feeling there is, even though I still haven't slept with a girl.

Challenge 6: Getting Physical

Rules:

(Minimum 1hr)

-Ask three girls for their phone number

-In at least 3 interactions you must initiate physical touch. (Any physical touch outside of a hug/handshake counts, and you can put your hand on her shoulder as a default.

Explanation

Being physical is a great way to show confidence and increase sexual attraction. But the primary purpose of this exercise is counterintuitive, it's about learning to be willing to go too far.

This doesn't mean being obnoxiously aggressive or intentionally creepy (i.e. don't grab at women's breasts), but one of the biggest reasons men don't get results in dating is that they're not willing to risk escalating with a girl because of the potential for awkwardness and rejection. They tell themselves they need to wait for 'the signal' to escalate an interaction, but it never comes, because they were really just rationalizing their fear of rejection.

Physicality allows you to get useful feedback. If a girl moves back or seems uncomfortable when you touch her, it's a red light, it means she's not comfortable with you yet and her guard is up. Take a step back whenever this happens. If this happens regularly, it indicates that you need to work on making women feel more comfortable around you.

If she accepts your touch, but doesn't reciprocate, it's a yellow light, she's comfortable with you, but she probably isn't interested in getting sexual with you yet, or she feels embarrassed because of the social context (she is around her friends, for example).

If she accepts your touch and she touches you back, it's a green light, she's comfortable with you and this is a sign that you can move the interaction forward (by kissing her for example). That said, she still could reject your advances, don't be offended if she does.

These signals give you feedback that allows you to adjust course and notice patterns of reactions which can help you find out what you may want to do differently.

Field report guidelines

For each interaction, ask yourself, did you initiate physicality? If not, what thoughts were holding you back? If so, how did it go? If you got a red light, why do you think that was? Did the rejection affect you? Were you uncomfortable touching a girl on the shoulder?

Example Field Report Challenge 6 Day 1

How many numbers did I ask for? 3

What did I do? Why?

I was excited on my way to campus, as I walked towards the food court, I noticed a stunning girl walking between classes, and I walked up and introduced myself. I started by asking where she was from, and the conversation ended up being about artificial intelligence somehow. She was cool, and I liked her quite a bit, but I didn't get the impression she was attracted to me. I used this as an excuse to not initiate any physical touch, I was afraid of getting rejected. I still asked for her number to get coffee with her, and went on my way. I was a bit frustrated with myself for not doing the challenge on the approach, but I used it as emotional fuel to push me forward.

I approached a girl who was sitting down and reading. I said, "I thought you looked very intriguing and I had to say hi." She was flattered and said thanks, but told me she had a boyfriend. I told her it was nice meeting her and moved on. I was actually in a better mood after this rejection. I didn't expect anything from her, I was offering value and expressing myself. I was proud of myself just for taking action. I'm doing this more for the thrill of it than anything else at this point.

I kept approaching for the next hour, and I kept putting off being physical, I was nervous about it because I felt it would make the rejection more 'real', I thought it would be awkward or cringey, and

I was afraid of that uncomfortable moment. The last girl I approached, I decided to suck it up and I touched her shoulder for a second before immediately withdrawing it. I felt very awkward for doing so, but she seemed fine with it. I was making it a big deal. I told her to have a good day before I walked home. Although I was a bit frustrated with my hesitation, I felt good about myself, I had a high from getting in a flow state. I hesitated with my physicality, but at this point, I know that hesitation is something I can get over with practice.

Challenge 7: Swapping Saliva

Rules:

(minimum 1hr 30)

-Ask at least 4 girls for their number each day.

-Initiate physicality with at least 2 girls.

-Attempt to kiss a girl each day

-You can use this line to attempt a kiss, "I can't help but want to kiss you right now." Afterwards, lean in.

Explanation

I used to have nightmarish daydreams about attempting my first kiss. I imagined being brutally rejected and shamed for trying. I imagined if I didn't get rejected, I would completely miss her lips, and that she would laugh at me for my failure.

Attempting a kiss puts you in a vulnerable position, and the thought of being rejected for a kiss can feel intimidating, but it's never actually a big deal. By learning to go for it, you can expect to get rejected some of the time, but at the same time if you never try, you're rejecting yourself.

Each time you get rejected for a kiss you will become more grounded and confident, and once you become comfortable with being rejected in this way, you will be shocked by what is possible.

Even if you're awkward when you lean in for the kiss, you're going to get more results than someone who is smooth but doesn't take risks. Even if a girl does reject your kiss, it often doesn't mean she is rejecting you, she's just not ready to kiss you yet. By showing her that you're willing to go for it, you can sometimes actually build attraction even if you get rejected. If you get rejected but don't give up you're showing a woman how attracted to her you are. You like her so much that you are willing to persist through rejection. However, there is a very important distinction that needs to be understood. If she is at all uncomfortable, you need to take a step back, if you persist then, you're just being creepy.

Field Report Guidelines

Note whether you get frustrated about hesitating. Write down your excuses if you don't go for it. Look for any rationalizations in those excuses.

If you get rejected, ask yourself what the consequences were, did you get upset? Did you feel awkward about it? Was it thrilling to take a risk? Did you make a big deal of the rejection?

When you leaned in for a kiss, what were your intentions? Did a part of you want to get rejected, or did you really want it to work? Why?

Example Field Report Challenge 7 Day 1

I skipped two days. I had to work extra hours, and I told myself going out wasn't a priority. But I played a couple hours of video games when I got home, so I know I was making an excuse.

I felt anxious on my way to campus today, the momentum I built up has diminished because of my days off. As I walked towards the food court, I started hesitating again, I told myself I needed to ease myself back into this (even though I know that the way out of anxiety is to take action). I spent about 15 minutes walking around before I saw a girl sitting down and I sucked up my anxiety to approach her.

I told her I thought she was cute, she thanked me and told me her name. I asked what she studied and we were getting along well. I was doing a good job of free flowing and being engaging. My eye contact was strong and I could feel sexual tension building. She said she had to go to class, and I asked for her number to get coffee the next day. She said yes, and walked away. I wanted to lean in for the kiss, even though I knew it was a bit awkward, just to see what would happen. I told myself I would do it next time, and brushed off my frustration at myself.

I kept approaching girls and I got in a flow state fairly quickly. The interactions were going well, I was maintaining strong eye contact and being physical. I repeatedly hesitated to lean in for the kiss, though. I made excuses like, "She's in a rush." "She seems like too nice a girl." "She doesn't seem to like me enough." Those excuses may have been accurate, but it's not about making out with girls as much as it is learning from rejection and getting out of my comfort zone.

I was feeling internal frustration because I wasn't pushing myself by going for the kiss. However, I did get several girls' numbers. Going for a kiss with someone I just met feels like a big deal, and like it could only end in embarrassment. But I don't know that. The only way to learn is through experience. I'm not going to be able to progress to the next challenge until I actually try, so each day I hesitate I'm putting it off further. I'm getting so close to getting the results I want, I just need to push myself a bit further.

Challenge 8: Sexual Healing

Rules:

-Continue challenge 7.

-Sleep with a woman you find particularly attractive.

Explanation:

I speak from experience when I say sleeping with someone just to validate your ego can be extremely unfulfilling. If your past is full of sexual frustration and feelings of inadequacy, there is a good chance you will latch on to this pattern, but having sex to prove yourself has consequences.

That isn't to say you shouldn't have casual sex, or that sex can't be done purely for the enjoyment of it. However, sex will be much more enjoyable when you are genuinely attracted to someone. This may seem glaringly obvious, but there is a common pattern for guys who try to improve this area of their lives. They start sleeping with girls they don't really like as 'practice' for the girls they do really like.

Be aware that having casual sex with someone you don't feel a connection with can do more harm than good. It's often a coping mechanism that doesn't work.

Don't consider this challenge completed until you have slept with someone who has a genuine emotional effect on you.

To initiate sex, you must get to a location where it's possible. Doing this doesn't have to be complicated, but you do want to be somewhat indirect. Saying, "would you like to come to my place and have sex?", puts a lot of pressure on a girl.
The excuse for going to your/her place can be simple like:

You: Hey, have you seen Donnie Darko?

Her: No

You: You have to see it, it's amazing Her:

Really? Okay.

You: Let's go watch it.

Her: Now?

You: Yeah, why not?

Her: okay.

If a girl is open to taking an interaction in a sexual direction, she won't need much convincing to get in a room with you. A friend of mine once told a girl that she really needed to see his book collection, and it worked.

Women are taught to be careful with their sexuality because they are so often judged for it. Many women will be uncomfortable if you are too direct, by suggesting a movie, you are taking the responsibility off of her.

In America, most women tend to be relatively open to sex without a commitment. However, some women won't be open to having sex on the first date, and some are waiting for marriage. This is a reality you must accept.

If a girl at any point says no or seems uncomfortable, you shouldn't be offended. And if you are frustrated by this, it shows that you are trying to 'take' sex from her, you see sex a 'prize', and you're not treating her like a human being, but like a sex object. This attitude may be correlated with the fact that she doesn't want to have sex with you, she can tell something's not quite right

Hopefully, you know how to have sex (if you don't, there are plenty of books on the topic available). However, I will give you some guidelines for escalating when you're in the bedroom.

1.   Don't rush it. When you start watching a movie you can put your arm around her, but escalate slowly. Give her time to get aroused. For her, foreplay is much more important than it is for you.

2.   Take steps back, when it starts to get hot and heavy, tease her by backing off. This will turn her on, and make her feel like she must earn the opportunity to have sex with you.

Field report guidelines

This challenge may take longer than the others, because you have to let go of a lot of your ego to be vulnerable enough to sleep with a woman you have strong feelings for. It can feel like a big moment, and it's not until you understand on an emotional level that it's not a big deal, that you'll be able to experience this. This lesson may take a good amount of trial and error.

Challenge 8 Day 1

What I did and why?

I went on a date with a woman who wouldn't have batted her eyelashes at me a few years ago. I thought she was completely out of my league, but I didn't use that as an excuse. I met her at a club a couple nights before and we hit it off amazingly well, I suggested we get coffee, and I was very excited that she was interested.

I was notably nervous waiting for her at the coffee shop, when I saw her, I hugged her, but I noticed I wasn't making strong eye contact because I was afraid of being vulnerable with her. I started telling myself that nothing would happen with this girl because I liked her too much, and I was nervous. Which, could easily have been a self-fulfilling prophecy.

The conversation was stilted for the first 5 minutes or so, I was judging myself rather than enjoying her company. I was trying to think of something good enough to say, I was trying to come off as 'cool', everything I did was a little bit fake.

After a few minutes, though, I started to get into the conversation. After about 20 minutes I noticed my eye contact was stronger, and I started to feel sexual tension building between us.

I suggested we go on a walk, after a few minutes of walking, I felt like I should try to hold her hand, but I was feeling hesitant. I kept thinking she might reject me, and I was worrying about how that rejection would feel, and what it would mean. But I knew my excuses were bullshit so I decided to go for it. We held hands, but I got so nervous that my hand would get sweaty that I let her hand go after only a few minutes.

We walked for about half an hour, and I knew I should be asking her to watch a movie, but I was feeling extremely hesitant. I asked her what movies she liked to ease into the topic, but I let myself get sidetracked, and I didn't actually invite her over.

At the end of the walk, I led her to my car. When we arrived, I said I had to go home and work (I did have work to do, but I was really just making an excuse), I held her next to me by the car and I told her, "I really like you."

She said, "I really like you, too."

I said, "I'm not going to kiss you yet, though.

She said, "Okay."

It was as lame as it sounds. I said I wasn't going to kiss her because this date was really important to me, and I didn't want to fuck it up with any risk taking.

We parted ways and on the way home I was pretty frustrated with myself for not going for it. At the same time, I couldn't have imagined going a date with a woman like that even a month ago.

I felt that I had ruined my chances with her, I started telling myself I needed to do better next time. Although I do want to take more risks next time, I can appreciate how far I've come.

Review

Now that you've finished reading *The Trial,* if you'd leave an honest review of this book on amazon, I would greatly appreciate it.

Action Taking Group

You're invited to beta-test (completely free of charge) a new type of coaching that I'm going to be launching soon.

The beta-test you're invited to is an action taking tribe. This is similar to the reddit seduction group or a forum, but it is much more powerful, exclusive, and it is completely oriented towards action-taking. (In fact- those who don't take action in real-life will be removed from the group.)

By the way: those who take the most action in this group will win weekly prizes. Prizes with real monetary value, and because your part of the free beta-test, you will never have to pay a dime for a weekly opportunity to win these prizes.

For example, the first week's first prize was two paperback books: Models: Attract Women Through Honesty by Mark Manson, and The Trial: Transform Your Dating Life In Eight Weeks by Avery Hayden.

So, you may be wondering what is this group, and how are prize winners determined?

The group is a tribe of action takers improving their dating lives, with a leaderboard acknowledging those who take the most action. Each day the leaderboard is updated, to start the following metrics are being measured:

1. Who went out and for how many hours.

2.   Number of women approached.

3. Most interesting interaction of the day.

These metrics were chosen because they apply to both newbies and advanced guys, those who rise to the top of the leaderboard (and win the weekly prizes) are those who take the most action.

I won't bog you down with the math, but the guy who takes the most action overall will win the weekly first prize.

(btw there will be a second and third prize winner who both win one eBook completely free of charge.)

So, what's the points of this group? To create a community of people who are taking real action. Too much of the seduction community is based on theory crafting and over analyzing (just check out the r/seduction front page for proof), this is an exclusive group for people who want to get real results in the real world.

Jim Rohn famously said, "You are the average of the five people you spend the most time with," there's a lot of truth to this statement, and this group, will help everyone involved be influenced by people who are taking action.

We will inspire each other by being updated on a daily basis about other people's action taking, we will be held accountable because every day, our 'stats' will be posted (whether you went out/did approaches etc), and a sense of friendly competition will be reinforced through the possibility of winning real-life rewards.

What's the downside? The downside is that if you don't take action, you will eventually be removed from the group- mental masturbation is strongly discouraged.

As an early beta-tester, you will have completely free lifetime-access to the group. Once the group is launched to the general public, it will require a monthly subscription for new members, but as an early beta-tester you will never have to pay a penny or give out your personal information.

The group is hosted by the application Facebook for a few reasons: it's completely free and works on all platforms (PC, Iphone, Android, etc.), it has great security, and nearly everyone already has an account.

BTW: The group is secret which means no one can see that you are in the group, nor can they see what you post in the group.

Follow this link to join the group: RPT Action Takers Group

Again, this is completely free to try and there's no risk, if you don't like it, you can simply leave the group, no questions asked.

Give it a try, be a part of a movement of guys who take action and are dedicated to changing their lives for the better.

All the best, Avery

About the Author

Avery Hayden is the author of <u>Zero Fucks Given</u>, <u>The Trial: Transform Your Dating Life in Eight Weeks</u>, <u>among others</u>. He lives in Arizona where he studied psychology and creative writing at the University of Arizona.

Because of his struggles with anxiety, he has been obsessed with psychology and self-improvement for many years. He believes there is a need for more self-improvement with a solid scientific foundation.

You can find free articles by Avery at: <u>https://redpilltheory.com/</u>

Other Books by Avery Hayden

Zero Fucks Given: The 21st Century Man's Guide to Deep Self-Confidence

The Seduction Blueprint

How to Conquer Social Anxiety: A Scientific, Step-By-Step Formula to Overcome Shyness, Break Free From Negative Thinking, and Unlock True Confidence

Appendix A

Finding Wings

Having other guys to go out with has many advantages. They can provide accountability and they can give you honest feedback to help you improve. In clubs, they can be helpful by distracting friends who could otherwise be an obstacle.

However, not having friends to go out with is not a valid excuse to put off doing the challenges. And, in many cases, wingmen are more of a crutch for each other than anything else. Most guys who go out don't push themselves much, they go out and hang out with each other more than they meet women, if you're not careful, their lack of action taking can influence you to take less action as well. Despite this, it's great to have friends to go out with. But it's important to be aware of the risk for laziness so you can proactively prevent it from happening.

There are Facebook groups run by the company Real Social Dynamics called inner circles, they are by far the easiest and most efficient way to find wingmen in whatever city you live in. Most cities have an inner circle group, and if your city doesn't, you can create one. To search for your city's inner circle, type, "RSD Inner Circle (name of your city)" into the Facebook search function, and request to join.

If you don't get accepted, send a direct message to a moderator and explain why you want to join (some moderators decline people by default). Post on the group that you're looking for people to go out with, and you should get some responses. If you don't, send direct messages to people in the group to find people to go out with.

Bonus Challenge 1: Setting a Frame

Rules:

-(45 minutes)

-Ask at least 3 women for their phone number

-Use the provided line in 3 interactions with women.

"I bet you don't meet someone like me every day."

Framing is a subtle psychological art, and when done right, can alter people's perceptions you. Research has shown the powerful effects framing can have; participants were given the task of singing karaoke in front of a crowd of strangers. The participants were, of course, highly anxious doing this and their performance suffered. Another group, however, had a different reaction. They were instructed to tell themselves they were excited whenever they noticed feelings of anxiety. Those who told themselves they were excited were notably less nervous than those who did not.

Creating the right frame in an interaction can evoke powerful emotions, and make you totally unforgettable.

Yeah, it's extremely cocky, but that's because overconfidence can be exceptionally attractive when done right. If you say this line with an insecure tone, it will seem like you are overcompensating, if you say it confidently, you'll be unforgettable.

This asserts a powerful frame into the interaction, you are saying that she doesn't get to meet someone like you every day, implying meeting you is an opportunity for her. It's also insidious because it proves itself true. Very few men would ever say something like this, so by doing so, you are proving that she doesn't meet guys like you every day.

The statement is also mysterious. It leaves room for interpretation, she'll want to know what it is that makes you different, why you would say something like that, even if she thinks you were being arrogant, you're so different that she will want to answer these questions. And to do so, she will have to see you again. If you want to make a strong impression on someone, make them think about you after you've met, and this line accomplishes that efficiently.

If you get bad responses to this line, it is signaling that you are overcompensating, and if you're overcompensating with this line, a week of consistent practice will help you to get comfortable with overconfidence and you will learn to deliver the line in a way that makes an impression women will never forget.

Guidelines

Write about how women reacted to your use of these lines, how did it affect their demeanor? If they reacted positively, ask yourself why it had that effect. If they reacted negatively, why do you think that happened? Did you feel nervous saying either of the lines? What did you think would happen?

Field report template:

How many girls' numbers did I ask for?

How many times did I use the line? "I bet you don't meet someone like me every day?"

What did I do and why?

Bonus Challenge 2: Teasing

Rules:

(min 45 minutes)

-Ask 3 women for their phone number

-Spike 3 girls' emotions by disagreeing with something they say.

Example:

If she says she is from California say, "I hate California." If she says she is a business major say, "I hate business." Alternative:

Instead you can say, "My grandpa likes California." Or, "My grandpa likes business," in a mocking tone.

Explanation

Modern men are raised to be people-pleasers. We are taught to be agreeable and to avoid even the slightest hint of confrontation. As pleasant as this makes conversation, it robs interactions between men and women of sexual tension.

Learning to be disagreeable in this way acts as an effective crutch to learn how to create sexual tension in a conversation. Practicing saying, "I hate x," allows you to get comfortable with challenging what a woman says, and if done well, can spark attraction.

Emotional spikes can sometimes offend, but even if a woman reacts negatively, you can ease her anger by apologizing and changing the subject.

Sometimes, an apology won't be enough, if she's still upset after your apology, you went too far, this usually indicates that you said the line in a genuinely confrontational tone, not a flirtatious or fun tone.

Once you are used to using this line, you will be less likely to filter out the challenging statements that naturally come to your mind, because tension is natural, but people-pleasing is trained.

Field Report Guidelines

In your field reports, analyze what you did differently when emotional spikes worked effectively and when they didn't. Also, track how your efforts to calibrate any bad reactions went and why they were effective or not.

Field Report Template

Date:

Emotional Spike Challenge Day 1

How many numbers did I ask for?

What did I do and why?

Made in the
USA
Monee, IL